From the Library of

Jean Hunt.

WARE'S PAST
IN PICTURES

WARE'S PAST
IN PICTURES

by
Maurice Edwards
and
David Perman

The Rockingham Press

First published 1991
by The Rockingham Press
11 Musley Lane,
Ware, Herts SG12 7EN

British Library Cataloguing in Publication Data

Ware's past in pictures
I. Edwards, Maurice II. Perman, David
942.5830014

ISBN 1 873468 04 0

Printed in Great Britain by
Bemrose Shafron (Printers) Ltd,
Chester

**Part of the proceeds of this book are donated to
the conservation work of The Ware Society**

Contents

Acknowledgements

The basis of this book is the collection of old postcards and snapshots, belonging to the town's conservation group, the Ware Society, which since about 1980 has been maintained on slides by Maurice Edwards.   The slides have been used by Maurice to give evening talks to many organisations and clubs, who have shown their appreciation by inviting him back again and again.   The collection has also provided the slide shows which add to the pleasure of the exhibitions in the Ware Museum.   One purpose of this book, therefore, is to give local people a permanent record of the enjoyable evenings they have spent listening to Maurice and watching the slides - not that he has any intention of giving up his talks.

The collection came into being through his friendship with Neil Jenkins, a past president of the Hertfordshire Postcard Club, who generously allowed copies to be made of his own photographs of old Ware.   From then onwards, the collection grew and grew.   It is impossible to mention here all the people who have come forward after Maurice's talks to lend their precious photographs to be copied.   We hope they will take this acknowledgement as conveying to them the warmest thanks of the Ware Society and of the authors.

Special mention, however, must be made of a few among the many who have lent us large and particular collections of photographs: Harry Adams, who worked for Ware U.D.C. in the 1930s, for *Nos. 15 and 101;* George Albany, a member of the barge-owning family, now living in Australia, for *Nos. 44, 45, 48, 49, 50, 51 and 62;* Don Clare, formerly of D. Wickham & Co Ltd, for *Nos. 87, 88, 91, 93, 94, 96 and 275;* Michael Evans, a former Secretary of the Ware Society, for *Nos. 8, 18, 24, 43, 149 and 168;* Mrs Pat Evans, the daughter of the late Charles Ballands, for *Nos. 142, 143, 262, 270 and 271;* Mrs Shirley Finn, formerly of D. Wickham & Co Ltd, for *Nos. 85, 86, 89, 90, 92 and 95;* Max Hoather for the early photograhs taken or copied from even earlier ones by his father, W.H. Hoather, *Nos. 39, 112, 160, 161, 168, 218 and 246;* Dr Bill May for the photographs of the 1947 floods taken by his son, Christopher May, *Nos. 137, 140 and 144;* Mrs Nan Murphy, the widow of Jerome Murphy, a local councillor and chief chemist for Henry Page & Sons, for *Nos. 111, 116, 120, 121, 122, 123, 124, 135 and 202;* Mick Ottley for the photographs of the 1988 Victoria Maltings fire, *Nos. 125 and 127;* Presdales School, Ware, for the use of *Nos. 231, 232, 233, 234 and 235;* Richard Shackle, who worked at Ware Library and copied many old photographs, for *Nos. 64, 104, 113, 115, 119, 173. 174, 199, 200, 208, 209, 211, 213 and 217;* and Ware Town Council for *Nos. 12, 192, 193, 194, 195, 196, 197, 198 and 244.*

We are also grateful to the Editor of the *Hertfordshire Mercury* for permission to use photographs *Nos. 267 and 272,* which remain the newspaper's Copyright, and to the Royal Commission on the Historical Monuments of England for permission to use their Copyright photographs *Nos. 118, 175, 203, 204 and 205* from the National Buildings Record.

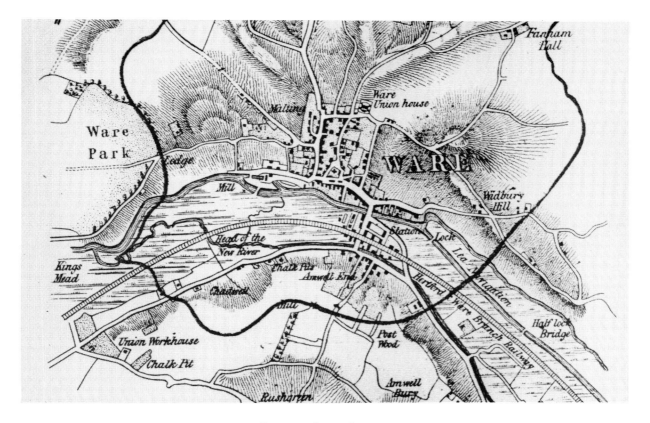

Introduction

Like most towns in Britain, Ware has seen major changes since 1945. Before the advance of the motor-car, many old buildings were demolished in road-widening schemes. More radical road schemes were planned in the 1960s and, though they were not implemented, still the buildings came down. Old industries disappeared and their sites were occupied by blocks of flats. And the High Street, which escaped the worst of the destruction, now has few of the family businesses that older people remember so fondly.

But Ware has been subject to constant change throughout its long history. Many of these earlier changes are outside the scope of this book because they occurred before the invention of photography. All the same, we can get glimpses of the more distant past as we picture the 19th and early 20th century town, since our forebears adapted and rebuilt rather than tending to demolish, as we do. Thus, the numerous Tudor inns in the High Street became town houses for merchants and maltsters, who later built maltings in their back yards and later still moved out of the town, leaving their houses to be converted into shops for the new middle classes.

The biggest change over the past 200 years has been the expansion of the town. The map shows Ware in 1849 restricted to a few streets on the north bank of the River Lea. Most of the south bank was still in the parish of Great Amwell. The break between town and country was sharp and not yet blurred by suburban development. But already the first middle class villas had appeared in New Road. Soon the new railway (built in 1843) would bring in more people and lead to new housing up the hillsides on every side of the town. We begin the book with a tour of the older part of the town.

Above: *1. Part of the map of Ware and Amwell End from the Public Health Report of 1849.*

Around the Town

Our first chapter takes us on a tour of the old town of Ware. We begin at the bottom of New Road and go along the High Street, looking back along East Street and West Street and down Priory Street. The street pattern was laid out by Ware's earliest Norman lords in the 12th century but gradually altered over the centuries. The old name for the south side of the street was Water Row, while the north side with all the buildings along the tops of East and West streets was known as Land Row. The buildings in between were known as Middle Row and were infilling - market stalls which became established as small houses. When the French Horn on the corner of Church Street (or "Dead Lane" as it was then known) was rebuilt in the early 17th century, it completed the process of narrowing the road.

Our tour then takes us northwards up Baldock Street, another part of the original town. We turn right along the Bourne, originally a narrow lane and a short cut round the back of the town. Crib Street was part of the old town, linking up with a lane which ran past Collett Hall and over Musley Common to Fanhams and also with the lane which ran eastwards to Widbury. We go down New Road (built as late as the 1830s) and at Bridgefoot, after pausing to look around, we cross the River Lea into Amwell End. This became officially part of Ware only in the 19th century. Before that, although long considered part of the town, it was in the parishes of Great and Little Amwell.

2.   *The eastern end of the High Street in 1908.*
3.   *The view from the bottom of New Road in the early 1900s.*

4.   *Aerial view of the High Street in the late fifties, with long maltings on every side.*

5.	The High Street and the corner of East Street in 1919.

6.	The French Horn still came to the corner of Church Street on this postcard of 1929.

7.	The centre piece of the Marketplace was the building known as the Town Hall, occupied here in 1899 by Stallabrass the butchers. It was built in 1827 as an arcaded cornmarket with a meeting hall above.

8.	A print of 1811 showing the old Tudor market hall, with the Bull's inn sign beside it. On the right is the French Horn without its brick facade.

9.	*The busy western end of the High Street in 1908, with Harradence's shop on the left, advertising Jaeger knitwear and "Achille Serre High Class Dyer and Cleaner."*

10.	*The view looking eastwards in the same year, with Brewster's and Culver's shops on*

11.   *St. Mary's Church in 1913. with the parish lock-up in front of it.   The railings on the left enclosed part of the churchyard and the War Memorial was not erected until June 1921.*

12.   *Also in front of the church were cottages and an old forge, which were demolished in 1937 to make way for the Memorial Gardens.*

13.   Above, West Street in the 1930s was a continuous row of 18th century and medieval houses. The first two brick cottages have now been demolished to make way for the Memorial Gardens. The next two have been restored and are now shops.

14.   Another view of West Street, from an etching of about 1900 by the Hitchin artist Frederick Landseer Maur Griggs.   In the centre of the picture is Churchgate House, at that time Edwards the bakers and now Richard Rainbow's motorbike shop.   This fine building, jettied on two sides, was built in the early 16th century as a house for the Chantry Priest, who served in St Mary's Church, which is seen in the background.

15. This snapshot, taken in the 1930s, shows 87 High Street (now the Library) with railings in front of it and 89 High Street (now demolished) bearing the sign "The Priory Hairdressing Saloon".

16. Priory Street (then called Mill Lane) in the early 1900s. In the centre of the picture is the old malting, which was the first premises of D. Wickham and Co, later the Ware Art and Technical School, and is now offices. The wall enclosed the orchard of the Priory, then a private house. The Lido swimming pool was built here in the 1930s.

17. *Baldock Street in 1908. On the left is the draper's shop of Horice Bigg, and beyond the two signs of the Golden Boot (Thomas Burgess the shoemaker) and the Royston Crow Public House. Opposite is the Bull's Head Inn, which is still there.*

18. *The last building before Watton Road was Percy Moss's cycle shop, pictured here in the 1960s. On the right is the Chequers Public House (now an estate agent's) and behind it the Star Brewery.*

19. *In 1908 the Hope Maltings occupied the west side of Baldock Street, where there is now a grass verge and the new fire station.*
20. *Thunder Hall, pictured here in 1908, was a Queen Anne House, heavily restored in 1850 with a new gatehouse, and now converted to flats as part of Thundercourt.*

21.   The entrance to the Bourne before it was widened in the early 1900s.

22.   Western House in Collett Road, photographed here in the 1930s, was originally the workhouse of the Ware Union, built in the 1830s.

23. *Crib Street, seen here from the churchyard in 1930s, was well provided with pubs. On the right is the Cabin and beyond it the Albion. Further up were the Red Cow and White Horse.*
24. *The top of Crib Street in the 1960s before flats were built on the right. The corner door at the beginning of Prince's Street was the entrance to the Prince of Wales Public House.*

25.   *Musley Hill, seen here on a postcard of 1905, was built in the 1840s as a continuation of New Road. The constable clearly had more leisure than today's policemen.*

26.   *Musley Lane, pictured in the early 1900s, was part of the old road leading out of Ware to Widbury and the Standard Pub was much frequented by farmers. In the distance is Trinity Road which was begun in the 1880s and overlooked the open fields of Musley Common.*

27. *New Road, seen here in 1908, was the town's first middle class street with spacious villas and four churches built in the 19th century.*

28. *At the bottom of New Road (also 1908) was the shop of A.H. Rogers, the printer and newsagent and also magistrate and staunch supporter of the Congregational Church in the High Street.*

29. *Endersby, the saddler and harness maker, and the Bridge Brewery and Barge pub in the 1900s. Note the narrow entrance to Star Lane, which was not widened until the 1916.*
30. *The High Street from Bridgefoot with the Star pub on the right.*

31. *A view of the tollbridge in 1896 from the window above Mayhew's grocery, later the Co-op.*
32. *Robert Stephenson's iron bridge pictured before the removal of the tollgate in 1873.*

Amwell End, Ware

Amwell End, Ware.

33. Amwell End in the 1920s with the Post Office on the right, and the Chapel in the distance.
34. The Spread Eagle and Leatherlands, when it was the Post Office in 1908.
35. Another view of Leatherlands, looking up Amwell End.
36. The railway crossing in the early 1900s. The small building on the left, between the railway and New River, had been the Post Office in the middle of the 19th century.

On the River

The river is the reason for the town's existence, for there has been a crossing here since pre-historical times. The Romans made a bridge here and built a small town beside Ermine Street. The Danes brought their ships up from the Thames to Ware and were defeated here by the Saxons under Alfred the Great. In the 13th century, the Lady of Ware Manor claimed tolls on all goods passing over and under the bridge, but had to compromise on the latter with the bailiffs of Hertford.

It has been known by various forms of its old Celtic name as the Lea, Lee, Lyge, Luy or called simply "Ware River". From Tudor times, the river was the main route for transporting Ware malt to the London brewers. Commercial barge traffic ended in about 1948, but the use of the river for leisure has continued. From the 18th century onwards, gazebos were established along the banks to offer Ware people and their guests a little peace and quiet away from the bustle of the High Street. The gazebos are now being restored.

37. *The river above the bridge at the turn of the century, with the maltings giving way to the gazebos, which looked out on open water meadows.*
38. *Down river in the 1930s. On the left is the huge corn dryer of Henry Page and Sons and opposite is the old building of Wickham's works.*

39. *A barge with sail aloft having just come under the iron bridge - a photograph from the 1890s.*

40. *Ware Mill in 1895 before it became part of Allen & Hanbury's factory. It is probably one of the two mills mentioned in Domesday Book.*
41. *The Old Fulling Mill which stood beside Ware Lock from a painting by John Varley in 1820.*

42. *Ware Lock from a postcard of 1916. In the background is Hope House, which was demolished by Glaxo in the 1980s to make way for a new manufacturing block.*
43. *The town's other mill photographed in 1967. The old building beside the Cut was built by J.W. French and Co in 1897 and the "Frenlite" silos in the 1960s. There had been a mill here for many centuries before.*

Opposite:

44. The wharf of C. Albany & Sons, off Star Street, in 1947.

45. Albany's iron barges, like these in 1947, had names beginning with the letters T, V and W. and had a shallower draft than other barges going down the Lea and on to the Thames.

Above:

46. An older timber barge, moored by the Victoria Cut in the early 1900s. On the stern is the name of the owner and the steersman, William Wilbourne.

47. Ware men were said to have warts on their chests from spending so much time leaning over the iron bridge.

48.   *During the Second World War, the London timber merchants Glicksten's, moved part of the country's strategic reserves out of London to Ware.   Here Will Adams, one of Albany's steersmen, is seen with a loaded barge in 1947.*

49.   *Timber being loaded on to barges beside the gazebos.*

Opposite:

50.   *The barge Windsor coming under Ware Bridge.*

51.   *Henry Butcher, the Albany's horseman, with friend.*

The Gazebos

The gazebos are a distinctive feature of Ware's river, and nowhere else in Britain does such a large group survive on a riverside. Early deeds show that a few existed in the late 17th century, but most date from the 18th and early 19th centuries. They were built by the innkeepers and owners of the High Street properties at the end of their gardens, to provide a quiet spot for leisure and refreshment away from the noise of the town. The journalist, James Smith, who spent his childhood in Ware in the 1830s, described them as "little Dutch summerhouses". In his time, there were 25 gazebos between the Priory and the Bridge, but neglect and planning blight had reduced their number to ten by the 1980s.

52. *"Summerhouses on the River Lea at Ware", a postcard of the 1920s.*

53. *"The Backs", an illustration in a magazine article in the 1900s.*

54. *A view of the gazebos down river, a photograph from George Price's book of Ware views printed by his company, The Ware Library, in 1908.*

55.   *The towpath and gazebos stretching westwards from a postcard of 1910.*

56.   *A similar view, with Guernsey cows grazing on the banks, from an advertising card for Allenbury's Infant Foods and Malted Rusks (the reverse is illustrated on page 51).*

River Lea
with back of
Maltings, Ware.

57.   *The fine two-storey gazebo behind No. 63 High Street and its watergate. The state of delapidation in 1981, when the Ware Society launched its initiative for their restoration. East Herts District Council took up the idea and three gazebos were restored with funds provided by the Council, the Ware Society and other bodies.*

58.   *The gazebo and watergate restored in 1984.*

White House Park, Ware.

Leisure on the river.

59.	*Members of the Harradence family in a punt opposite their garden in the 1890s.*
60.	*The White House, formerly the Cat and Monkey pub, between Ware and Hertford, where punts could be hired and a ferry operated in the early 1900s.*
61.	*Diving off the greasy pole at the Foresters' Gala in the 1900s.*
62.	*A horse-drawn sledge on the frozen Lea in 1901.*

63.   *A furniture remover's van in Gladstone Road before 1914.*

64.   *A brewer's cart outside the brewery in West Street.   On the right is Mr Edwards, the baker, and behind his shop, later known as Jaggs and Edwards.*

Road and Rail

The way through Ware - up Amwell End, the High Street and Baldock Street - formed the Old North Road from London to Scotland. Chaucer mentioned it in *The Canterbury Tales,* and the armies of medieval England used it. In Tudor times it was a busy highway, with Ware becoming one of the country's first posting towns. But in the 17th century the passenger coaches had to compete with the lumbering wagons of the malting industry, sometimes drawn by as many as five horses, which churned up the road. The result was England's first turnpike, erected at Wadesmill in 1666.

The road through the town did not become part of the turnpike system until 1725, when it was included in the Cheshunt Turnpike which lasted until 1873. In 1843, the Eastern Counties Railway put rails across the turnpike in Amwell End and had to divert the turnpike along Viaduct Road. In modern times, the road formed part of the A10 until the by-pass was built across the Meads in 1976.

65. *Two malting carts in Amwell End in about 1910.*

66. *An 18th century print of the Wadesmill toll-gate.*

67. Mr Castle, the Baldock Street baker, in his cart behind the Punch House in 1910.

68. Delivering milk from a horse-drawn float outside Ware.

69. Ware had a number of wheelwrights in the days of horse-drawn traffic, like this one in Baldock Street before 1914.

70. The motor-car brought new businesses to the town, like Gideon Talbot's filling station and repair shop in the High Street, seen in the 1940s. It was demolished in the 1960s to make way for a Tesco's store.

Showing off new motor-cars.

71. *Steam cars in the 1890s outside Has and Company in Amwell End (now a news-agent's).*

72. *A Model T Ford and carts outside Ware Garage in the early thirties.*

73. *An array of saloon cars outside Ware Garage in 1914.*

74. *Roadsters on display in the yard of the Saracen's Head in 1906.*

The railway arrived in Ware in 1843 after much debate and controversy. There had been an earlier proposal to run the London to Cambridge main line through the town, but this was defeated by the local landowners. In 1841, a parliamentary bill was passed to bring a branch line from Broxbourne through Ware to Hertford East, but the Cheshunt Turnpike Trustees stressed the "extreme danger and inconvenience to the public of allowing the railway to cross the Turnpike" at Amwell End - a view which modern drivers and pedestrians would surely endorse!

Protracted negotiations followed between the Eastern Counties Railway Company, the Turnpike Trustees, the River Lee Navigation and the New River Company. These resulted in a single track crossing Amwell End, and the Railway agreeing to divert the Turnpike along Viaduct Road and rebuilding the river bridge. This iron bridge was designed by the Railway Company's superintendent engineer, Robert Stephenson.

75.   *An early bus of the 1920s. Ware's first bus service was run by the People's Motor Services, begun by Mr W.L. Thurgood in 1927, and later compulsorily purchased by the London Passenger Transport Board. Mr Thurgood went on to found Jersey Airways and a coach-building factory in Park Road and to manufacture plastic panels of "Wareite".*

76.   *Cabs and hotel carriages in 1910, waiting outside Ware Station, then part of the Great Eastern.*

77.   *Ware Station in 1908. A footpath ran across the tracks from the bottom of Hoe Lane, so that passengers did not have to make a long detour if the crossing gates were closed.*

78. *A Hertford East train in Ware Station in 1957.*

79. *No 69652 passing the old signal box at the end of the platform in the 1950s.*

80.   The station-master and eleven others who formed the staff in 1926, controlling not only the passenger traffic but also extensive goods sidings.

81.   The engine shed and goods sidings in the 1950s. In the background can be seen the Victoria Maltings and Frenlite Flour Mill.

82.   *An aerial view of the Allen & Hanbury's works from the Ware Town Guide of 1927.*

83.   *The converted mill and works in 1912.*

Ware at Work

From Tudor times, Ware was an industrial town. The main industry was malting, which is dealt with in the next chapter. But many other industries grew up alongside malting. Some of them, like brickmaking and engineering, were connected with the malting trade. Others came in to take advantage of the town's good communications, plentiful water supply and large labour force.

Allen and Hanbury was founded in 1715 in the City of London and became leading manufacturers of surgical instruments and medicines. In 1898, they acquired the old mill in Mill Lane (now Priory Street) and built a factory there - it is said because one of their directors was a keen fisherman and came to Ware in the footsteps of Izaak Walton. In Ware, the manufacture of pharmaceutical products continued as well as special foods for infants and invalids, as can be seen in the advertisement to the right. Allen and Hanbury became part of the Glaxo Group in 1958 but continued to trade under its own name until 1978. Glaxo have now rebuilt the site in Priory Street and established a large research centre on the other side of Harris's Lane.

84. Allen and Hanbury's workers packaging medicines at Ware in 1926.

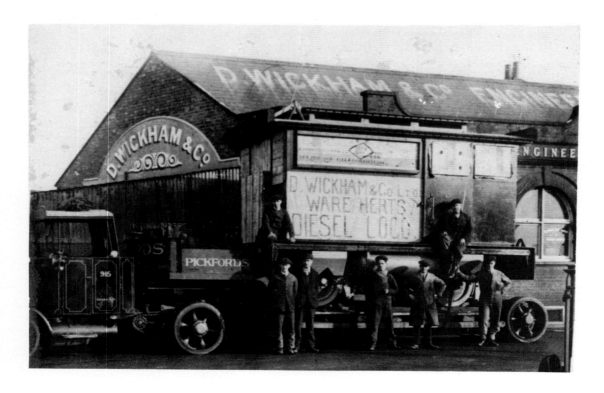

93. *Winston Churchill, sitting on a Wickham's No 17 gang trolley during the Second World War.*

94. *Workers testing a gang trolley after the war.*

95. *A group of Wickham's workers in 1939.*

96. *Loxley ("Rodney") Ford, who joined Wickham's as an apprentice in 1919 and retired as the works director in 1987. Ten years earlier, he had received the Queen's Silver Jubilee Medal for services to the engineering industry.*

97. The brickfields, seen here in the 1900s, were beside the river above Ware Lock, on a site now occupied by Glaxo's sports ground.

98. The gravel pits in Watton Road (now occupied by Wulfrath Way) were owned by William Skipp, who also founded Ware Garage and built the town's first cinema in 1911.

99. A 1928 lorry belonging to the J.W. French & Co.

100. French's Frenlite lorries in Kibes Lane during the 1950s.

101. *Piling for the Lido swimming pool in Priory Street, built by Ware Urban District Council in 1934. Left to right: Harry Adams, resident engineer for Ware U.D.C., Mr Whitehorn, highways foreman, and Mr Hyatt, Assistant Surveyor of Ware Rural District Council.*

102. *C. Smith, Monumental Mason, in Amwell End in the 1930s.*

103. *Laying a gas main in Baldock Street in the 1920s, with the foreman, Mr Newton, centre.*

104. *Ware had manufactured its own town gas from coal since 1830 and lit the High Street with it. The gas was stored in this gasholder in Bowling Road, seen here in 1968.*

105. *The Falcon Works, run by the Goodfellow family, supplied ironwork to the malting industry (a photograph from the "Pictorial Record" of 1899).*
106. *Pavey's bakery carts in Musley Hill.*

107. *Horace Page delivering for the New Road Dairy in the 1920s.*
108. *F. Cutmore of New Road was a decorator, sanitory worker and undertaker into the bargain. The building is now an art gallery.*

The River Lea, Ware.

A Malting Town

Malting is the process of turning grain, usually barley, into a form of sugar called maltose, which is the raw material of the brewing industry. This is done by allowing the grain partially to germinate and then curing and roasting it on a kiln. The malting industry was the backbone of Ware's economy for over 300 years. There are records of maltsters in operating in the town during the Middle Ages, but it was in the 1600s - when major breweries were established to cater for the expanding populace of London - that malting really took over the town.   At the beginning of the 18th century "brown malt" was discovered - probably by accident when someone allowed the kiln fire to flare up and probably in Ware. This became the raw material for the brewing of a popular stout known as "porter" or "entire", and many Ware maltings were exclusively devoted to it. For the next 150 years, the town became the premier malting supplier to the London brewers with the price of Ware malt being separately quoted on the markets of the metropolis. Pigot 's Directory for Hertfordshire in 1823, observing that immense quantities of malt were conveyed to London by river, said "perhaps there is not a town in England in which more malting business is done."

109. *The Omega Maltings between the river and Star Street, now converted into flats.*
110. *Henry Page and Company's corn-dryer from a postcard of the early 1900s.*

111. *A typical Ware skyline - Henry Page and Company's No. 27 and 28 brown maltings behind Crib Street and behind them the large 19th century No 22 malting, which was destroyed by fire in 1961, while being used to store radio and television sets.*

112. *Two workers outside the kiln of Henry Ward and Sons' malting behind 37 High Street*

113. *Four Ware maltmakers, wearing moleskin trousers tied at the knees - it is said to prevent the rats running up them. Note the cat hole in the door.*

114. *Nine maltmakers, photographed in 1912, with the tools used in the traditional malting process. Behind the seated man are faggots of hornbeam, used on the kilns for making brown malt.*

115. *A maltmaker cycling down Star Street in the early morning in the 1950s - the kilns were usually lit by 5 a.m.*

116. The extensive Crib Street maltings, seen from New Road and overlooking Deerfield, where the Croft family kept their deer.

117. Henry Ward's maltings on the north side of Star Street, photographed in the 1960s. The site is now occupied by flats.

118. The Canons Malting, off the Wadesmill Road, dated from at least the early 17th century. It was demolished to make way for new housing.

119. Nearer the town centre in Baldock Street was the Hope Malting, photographed here in 1962.

Ware's biggest malting firm was that of Henry Page & Company. It was built up from a relatively small local business by Henry Page, who in 1880 wrote to Gladstone as Chancellor of the Exchequer, protesting at the abolition of the malt tax and saying that "single handed I pay more Duty than any other Maltster".

120. Henry Page's house at 87 High Street (now the Library) with the firm's offices next door.

121. Henry Page, 1813-1894.

122. The Victoria Malting, built by the firm in 1907 to replace an earlier building and in its time the largest malting in England.

123. The new silo and corn dryer built beside the Victoria Malting in 1950 and now part of the completely automated plant of Paul's Malt.

124. *The malting industry stand at the Ware Exhibition of Trades and Hobbies, held in the Drill Hall, Amwell End, in 1950. Shortly afterwards, the four surviving malting firms in Ware and Hertford were amalgamated and then sold to Pauls and Sandars of Ipswich (now Pauls Malt).*
125. *The fire which destroyed the disused Victoria Malting on September 16th 1988.*

126. *The Victoria Malting before the fire.*
127. *A fireman on a hoist dousing the embers on the morning after the fire.*

Fire and Flood

As the last chapter showed, fire was a constant hazard in Ware's timber-built maltings, particularly if the kiln fire flared out of control. The town did not get a proper fire brigade until after 1849 and the establishment of the Local Board of Health (forerunner of the Urban District and Town Councils). Before then, fire-fighting was a haphazard affair. The churchwardens of St. Mary's kept a fire engine in a building in Church Street but before it could be used the horses had to be rounded up on Crane Mead and harnassed to the contraption. Other engines were maintained by the insurance companies, usually in Hertford, and their firemarks were put on buildings.

128. *Flames engulfing the original Victoria Malting in 1906.*

129. *The shed against the wall of the churchyard in Church Street, where the Ware Brigade's fire escape was kept.*

130. *The Brigade in attendance at the Victoria Malting fire in 1906.*

131. *An 18th century firemark in New Road.*

132.   *The Brigade and its new steam pump at Buryfield in 1912.*

133.   *Captain J. Hart (right) and the Brigade with their new Merryweather motorised engine and trophies outside the Priory in the 1930s.*

134. *The Ware Brigade after a fire in 1906.*

135. *The spectacular fire which burned the corn dryer in Star Street in 1947.*

Railway Flooded at Ware, Herts, 1903.

Flooding was the other major hazard in Ware from time immemorial. Early historians record that in 1408 the town was almost destroyed "by the great inundation of waters that from the upland pass by the town". Within living memory, some flooding occurred in most years and there were serious floods in 1947 and 1968, when the Lea broke its banks. In 1974 the Thames Water Authority deepened the river to run between brick and metal walls and established by-pass sluices at Ware and Hardmead locks.

136. *A postcard of 1903 showing the railway tracks flooded.*

137. *Inundated fields beside the railway in the serious floods of 1947.*

138. *A postcard of Amwell End flooded in 1903.*

139. *A detail showing Mr Leatherland outside his shop in 1903.*

140. *Amwell End flooded in 1947, as seen from the side of the Victory pub near the bridge.*
141. *The flooded cottages in Amwell End in 1947.*

142. *The waters lapping the foyer of the Astoria Cinema in 1968.*
143. *The view up Amwell End during the 1968 floods.*

144. *Star Street flooded in 1947 when the old course of the River Lea overflowed its banks. In the distance is the Angel Public House.*

145. *The Star Street floods of 1947. On the right is the Victoria Public House.*

146. *Trying to repair the broken bank of the river in 1947.*

147. *Pile-driving as part of the flood alleviation scheme in 1974. The work added further deterioration to the neglected gazebos.*

Shopkeepers

Like other old towns, Ware has had shops for centuries. But modern shops, as we know them, with their prominent name plates, elaborate window displays and advertisements, were a Victorian invention. The coming of railway and the building of middle class housing outside the town centre provided the customers for many such shops in Ware, in particular the drapers, grocers and butchers, who displayed their goods outside their shops without too much attention to hygiene.

148. *John Page's Forage Stores at 96 High Street was covered with advertisements in the 1920s.*

149. *A related business, William Page & Son, photographed in 1967 and still in business at 31 High Street. The Pages were originally corn and coal merchants and had a wharf on the river.*

150. *Cooper's the tobacconist at 34 High Street (now a restaurant) photographed in the 1890s.*

A Spread of Drapers: the retailing of cloth and clothing - in every shape and form from linen sheets to underwear and the livery uniforms of servants - was an important part of the Ware shopping scene. The oldest draper's shop was Harradence's department store, which occupied the buildings at 65-73 High Street. It was founded in 1775 and proudly claimed that it had served Ware through the reigns of nine monarchs before it closed in the 1960s. But it had many rivals as these pages show.

151. Charles G. Randle was a linen draper at 84 High Street (Gilpin House) in 1899. The shop became the Blue Boot Stores in 1903, was later a furniture store and is now Tarling's DIY shop.

152. Charles Forbes's shop at 54 High Street in the 1930s.

153. Harradence's store and delivery van in 1907.

154. A 1906 advertisement for Grover's at 32 High Street.

155. A 1906 advertisement for Harradence's.

156. *61 High Street has been a chemist's shop since the mid-18th century when it ceased to be an inn. Mr Samuel Parkes Woollatt was later joined by Mr Coggin to form the name of the present shop. This drawing was on a Christmas card sent to customers in the 1940s.*

157. *An advertisement for Woollatt's Corn Cure from a book of Ware photographs published in 1908.*

158. *The Enfield Highway Co-operative Society took over an existing grocer's shop at 12 High Street in the 1920s, and then rebuilt it to form the present shopfront.*

159. *The International Stores at 42 High Street, seen here in the 1930s, was one of two chain stores present in Ware. The Home and Colonial occupied Stallabrass's former shop in the old Town Hall.*

The evolution of a grocer's shop:

Opposite:

160. Giffin's - "The People's Tea, Grocery and Provision Stores" - was established in Ware at the beginning of the 19th century, first in Baldock Street and later at 39 High Street. Ebenezer Giffin was the owner in the early 1900s when this photograph was taken by his nephew, the Bushey photographer W.H. Hoather. Note the frock coat.

161. Ebenezer's father, Samuel Giffin, posed in stove-pipe hat for this photograph taken in the 1880s. He died in 1886, aged 88 years.

This page:

162. After Ebenezer Giffin's death in 1909, the shop was bought by William H. Cullen, who traded there until the end of the Second World War. This photograph was taken before 1914, when some of the shoppers still wore Victorian dress.

163. After the Second World War, the shop became Swain & Nickolds (pictured here in the 1960s), and later the Epicure Delicatessen, owned by Mr and Mrs Hays-Palmer. After the building of Tesco's Store next door, it became the showrooms of the Eastern Electricity Board.

Butchers and Poulterers:

This page:

164. Mr Brewster, poulterer and fishmonger, at 79 High Street, pictured in the 1900s.

165. W.G. Clark & Sons at 33 Amwell End was established in 1835 and used to slaughter their own meat behind the shop. It became a kebab take-away in 1989.

Opposite:

166. A Christmas display at the Stallabrass Brothers' shop in the old Town Hall, in the early 1900s.

167. Another Christmas display in 1908, by J.R. Taylor, "Purveyor of High Class Meat", next door to the Saracen's Head Hotel.

Inns and Pubs

Ware has always been well endowed with licensed premises. When licensing was first introduced in 1552, Ware was an important coaching stop on the Old North Road and on the south side of the High Street alone there were 16 inns, side by side. Later alehouses and beer retailers, catering for the maltmakers, added to the number of pubs. In 1906, the town had more licensed premises per head of population than any other urban district in Hertfordshire. There are pictures of the former inns and pubs of Ware throughout this book. On these page are the pubs which stood on the north side of the High Street.

168. *In West Street, the original north side of the High Street, were the Punch House, Bell and Sun and White Swan - a picture taken in 1967.*

169. *In East Street (seen here in 1908) were the Crown and Anchor, Dolphin and Plough.*

170. *Beyond in New Road was the Red Lion, pictured in the 1960s.*

171. *The Market Square (photographed in 1908) was surrounded by inn signs: on the right are the French Horn, the John Barleycorn, Lion and Wheatsheaf and White Swan, and (centre picture) at the other end of the Town Hall the sign of the Oriental Tavern.*

Saracen's Head Hotel, *FAMILY & COMMERCIAL*

Telephone : Ware 118   High Street, Ware, Herts.

FRONT OF HOTEL

REAR VIEW

On the south side of the High Street, formerly called Water Row, stood the most important old inns of Ware. Evidence of them can still be seen in the waggonways, which opened on to the innyards.

One of the oldest of these inns was the Saracen's Head, opposite the bottom of New Road. When it was demolished in 1958 to make way for road-widening, it was realised what a loss this had been to the town's heritage. A massive crown post roof, Elizabethan wallpaintings and a Regency staircase were revealed. Medieval documents recently discovered show that the Saracen's Head dated back to at least 1364. It was also the last resting place in the town of the Great Bed of Ware.

172. A postcard for the Saracen's Head from the 1920s. On the reverse someone has written: "please can we have a lettuce".

173. The yard behind 65 High Street, formerly the Christopher Inn.

174. The yard behind 51 High Street, formerly the Bear and before that the Falcon Inn.

Above:

175. The Old Brewery Tap (photographed in 1942) is the last surviving pub in what used to be Water Row. It was rebuilt in the Regency period, but has a medieval doorway and cellars. In the reign of Elizabeth I, it was the Horseshoe and it has also been known as the White Horse, Golden Cross, New Crown and Crown and Star, as well as being the private dwellings of a curate and the manager of a brewery.

176. *The regulars of the Victory in Amwell End, before their day out by charabanc to the Newmarket Races in the 1930s.*

177. *On the opposite corner of Amwell End stood the Bull, which had stables for barge horses.*

178. *The Cherry Tree was midway down the east side of Amwell End.*
179. *The Red House (now a garage) was one of a number of pubs at the entrance to the town on the London Road, including the Malakoff, the "Johnny Gilpin" and the Royal Oak.*

Rich and Poor

A hundred years ago, the contrast between the town's rich and the poor was dramatic. By the 1890s, most of the wealthier citizens had built themselves large houses in spacious parkland outside the town. The labouring classes, drawn to Ware by employment in the malting industry or on the barges, lived in crowded yards, which clustered around Amwell End and Baldock Street. The Public Health Report of 1849 revealed appalling sanitation in these yards and a level of infant mortality and life expectancy which could be compared with industrial Lancashire. However, Ware's richer citizens did not turn their backs on this poverty; charity was dispensed daily at the large houses and a number of important buildings were endowed by the landowners.

180. *The Long Gallery of Fanhams Hall, rebuilt in 1901 by Mrs Croft, daughter of the maltster Henry Page.*

181. *Mrs Croft's husband, Lieutenant Richard Benyon Croft RN, and their sons, Richard Croft and Henry Croft (later an M.P., member of Churchill's war time Cabinet and created Baron Croft).*

182. *Fanhams Hall from the gardens.*

183. *Mrs Anne Elizabeth Croft, who in 1920 leased the Priory to the townspeople of Ware for 999 years at three shillings (15p.) a year.*

The Priory was built in the 14th century as a religious house of Franciscan Greyfriars or Friars Minor. (It should really be called the Friary, so as not to confuse it with the Benedictine Priory which existed in another part of the town.) After Henry VIII's Dissolution of the Monasteries, it became a private house, with extensive grounds including a wooded island. A number of families lived here in the 19th century, until it was bought by Mrs Croft in 1913 who allowed it to be used as a hospital during the First World War and then gave it to the town.

184. *The Priory seen from the river in a print of 1811.*

185. *The Priory gates at the High Street entrance, which were removed in the 1950s and then mysteriously disappeared.*

186. *The drawing room of The Priory from the 1913 sale catalogue. The central wall was later removed to form a large meeting hall.*

187. *A fancy dress portrait of Sir Martin Le Marchant Hadsley Gosselin, the distinguished diplomat, who spent his childhood in the Priory.*

188. *Amwell House was rebuilt in the 1760s by the Quaker poet John Scott, and had a large garden containing the famous grotto. This print is of 1811, when the poet's daughter, Mrs Maria Hooper, lived here. She was a great benefactress of the poor of Amwell End and established a school on her property. The house became the Ware Girls' Grammar School in 1906 and is now part of Ware College.*

189. *Ware Park, rebuilt in the 1880s by William Parker, who gave part of the Buryfield to the townspeople as a recreation ground.*

190. *Poles, the large country house at Thundridge, rebuilt by Robert Hanbury in the 1870s. It later became a convent school and has now been converted into the Hanbury Manor Hotel.*

191. *Robert Hanbury, 1798-1884, chairman of the brewers Truman, Hanbury and Buxton, who financed the new Thundridge church and gave the land on which Christ Church, Ware, and its school and vicarage were built.*

For centuries the labouring classes of Ware lived in crowded yards off Amwell End and Baldock Street, and in equally poor housing nearer the town centre, in Kibes Lane and Bluecoat Yard. The 1849 Public Health Report described the appalling conditions of the yards. A "slum clearance" programme was begun in the 1930s by the enterprising Surveyor to Ware Urban District Council, Robert Grantham, although the final demolition of the yards was not completed until only after the Second World War. The people were finally rehoused in new council houses on the King George's estate and near Watton Road. These pictures are from the photographic record made in the 1930s by Ware U.D.C.

Opposite:

192. *Cherry Tree Yard, off Amwell End. The 1849 Public Health Report said that the six yards on the east side of Amwell End contained 70 tenements with very poor sanitation.*
193. *Wash day in nearby George Yard, in 1935.*

Above:

194. *Kibes Lane, seen from New Road in 1935, with the Old Harrow public house on the left and the Jolly Bargeman farther down on the right (both pubs were later relocated on the King George's Estate). The Public Health Report said that "nearly half the cases of cholera in Ware in the year 1832 occurred in Kibes Lane."*

195.   *Chapel Yard on the western side of Amwell End, which contained 28 houses.*

196.   *Mrs Skeggs in Caroline Court, one of the most notorious yards off Baldock Street.*

197. *Hunter's Yard, the most southerly of the Amwell End yards.*

198. *The Hammond family gather with their animals in Cherry Tree Yard.*

Demolition

Apart from a stick of bombs dropped on New Road, Ware escaped serious damage during the Second World War. But in the 30 years which followed the peace, a great many of the town oldest and fine t buildings were demolished. Soon after Nikolaus Pevsner wrote his Hertfordshire volume in the *The Buildings of England* series, many of the buildings he had praised were razed to the ground. The pretexts for bringing in the bulldozers were very different from that which motivated Mr Grantham's slum clearance of the thirties. The commonest causes were road widening and making way for new road schemes, which often did not take place.

The biggest threat to the old town came in the mid-sixties with the Hertfordshire County Surveyor's proposal for a dual carriageway Inner Relief Road to run from Viaduct Road to Watton Road. Associated with this road plan was a proposal for a Central Area Redevelopment, which would have created a civic centre north of the High Street. Neither plan was implemented, but the resulting "planning blight" led to the eventual demolition of many buildings. The Ware Society was formed in 1965 to fight this orgy of destruction, but it was not until 1974 that most of the old buildings of Ware were "listed" and received some form of statutory protection.

199. *The row of timber-framed buildings at Bridgefoot, photographed in the 1950s just before their demolition so that the bridge could be widened.*

200. *The old cottages on the west side of Amwell End, demolished in the fifties and replaced by modern shops with flats above them.*

201. *The Saracen's Head, one of Ware's oldest inns, just before its demolition in October 1957.*

202. *A stone mullioned window at the Canons Malting in Wadesmill Road, which was demolished in 1965 by Ware U.D.C. to enlarge an adjoining housing estate. Below the window was a brick with the inscription, "IC 1622", which underlined the protests of those who tried unsuccessfully to save this old malting.*

203. *The Grange at the corner of Hoe Lane was demolished in August 1972 so that the London Road could be widened. Behind the dull Victorian facade was concealed a timber-framed house of great antiquity.*

204. *The Corn Stores in Star Street which were demolished in 1960 to make way for a warehouse which has now been replaced by flats. Pevsner in 1953 commented that the survival of such a large commercial building from the 17th century was very rare indeed. It is said that Cromwell's troops were quartered here during the Civil War.*

205 *A view of the interior of the Corn Stores.*

Opposite:

206. Cottages near the beginning of Church Street, which were demolished as part of the Central Area Redevelopment and replaced by a garage showroom.

207. Other cottages in Church Street demolished in the 1960s and now replaced by the entrances to a carpark and a small industrial estate.

This page:

208. Demolition taking place at the corner of Church Street and Crib Street.

209. A house and cottages in Crib Street, which were saved from demolition, but became so blighted that they too came down.

210. *Hope Malting and the maltster's house, at the corner of Baldock Street and Watton Road, demolished in 1969 to accomodate a large roundabout.*

211. *Percy Moss's shop on the opposite corner of Watton Road, which also came down.*

212. *Across Baldock Street, at the entrance to Monkey Row, was a large Tudor building, divided between a bakery and the home of Miss May Savidge. Miss Savidge, a retired technical illustrator, had lived there for 20 years and fought hard to save the whole building from demolition. But Ware U.D.C. acquired the bakery by compulsory purchase and then came the threat of the Inner Relief Road. But still Miss Savidge was not defeated. She had the building dismantled and numbered the 1000 oak timbers for re-erection elsewhere. The picture, from a feature about her in the magazine Titbits, shows her at work rebuilding the house at Wells-next-the-Sea, Norfolk, in 1978.*

210. *The bakery which was part of the building Miss Savidge took to Norfolk.*

214. *Demolition of houses in front of the Priory in 1967 as part of the Ware U.D.C.'s policy of "opening up" the High Street (a photograph by May Savidge).*

215. *"Ware Library" at 43/45 High Street was formerly the 17th century Flower de Luce Inn. Along with the neighbouring building (formerly Gideon Talbot's shop, illustrated on page 43) it was demolished in the 1960s and replaced by the town's first Tesco store.*

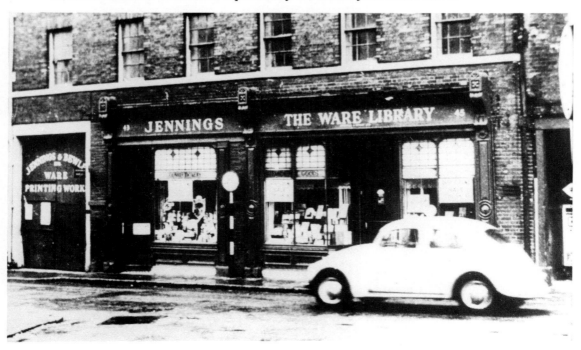

216. *Demolition taking place in about 1970 of the three maltings on the north side of Star Street, formerly operated by Henry Ward and Sons. They were replaced by a warehouse, and then by flats.*

217. *A range of late medieval cottages in Baldock Street, which were demolished in 1973, despite being listed. On the right is the Tudor gateway of the former Black Swan Inn.*

ST MARY'S CHURCH, WARE, HERTFORDSHIRE
To the Rev᷎ the Master & the Fellows of Trinity College Cambridge.
This Engraving is respectfully Dedicated by their obedient Servant J.C.Carter.

Ware at Prayer

Throughout its history, the town has been noted for both drink and piety - the number of its well-filled pubs and well-filled churches. During the Middle Ages there were two churches - the parish church, served at first by Benedictine monks, and the Franciscans' church on the opposite side of the High Street. In the 17th century, the town became strongly Protestant in its faith: an Independent Chapel was established in 1662 and a Friends' Meeting House soon afterwards, with other denominations, like Baptists, meeting in people's houses. But it was the Victorians who built the most churches, as the following pages show.

Opposite:

218. *The interior of St Mary's in the 1890s, with texts and commandments painted on the walls and the pulpit on the left. It was heavily restored in 1849, 1885 and again in 1905.*

219. *The clergy, churchwardens and numerous choir members at St Mary's pose in the churchyard in the 1930s.*

Above:

220. *The parish church before its drastic restoration in 1849 by the Gothic revivalist architect, George Godwin. The engraving is respectfully dedicated to the Master and Fellows of Trinity College, Cambridge, who became patrons of the living in the reign of Henry VIII.*

221. Christ Church was built in 1858 to form a second Anglican parish in the town. From the outset, it was an Evangelical parish, tackling the major social problems of the town, such as poverty and drink.

222. The girls of Christ Church Sunday School in 1910.

223. The large Catholic Apostolic Church (now converted to housing) was built in 1856 by the "Irvingites" with seating for 130 people. Two doors away, behind 50 New Road, was the Zoar Strict Baptist Church.

224. The Wesleyan Methodists built their first church in New Road in 1838 and enlarged it in 1886. In 1978, they joined with the United Reformed Church to form the Leaside Church, and their building became the Full Gospel Church.

Opposite:

225. *The Independents (Congregationalists) were in Ware in 1662 but their earliest surviving building is the chapel in Church Street, which was built in 1778. It had a three-decker pulpit, seating for 450 people and numbered among its ministers William Godwin, who became a famous free-thinker. Worship there ceased in 1918. The building later became a club and an auction room, and is now used as a small factory.*

226. *There were Quakers (Friends) in Ware in the 17th century. In 1661, 13 of them were imprisoned in Hertford Castle for refusing to swear an oath of loyalty to the king. They met at first in people's houses, but a meeting house was built in 1777 on land given by David Barclay of Youngsbury. This was tucked away behind the houses in Kibes Lane, and nearby was the Quakers' burial ground, containing over 200 graves. The Meeting House closed in 1881, after the death of its main supporter Mrs Hooper, the daughter of the poet John Scott. Our picture shows the burial ground in 1897, now a grassed area in the middle of a carpark.*

Above:

227. *The Congregational Church in the High Street was founded in 1816 after a dispute among the worshippers in Church Street. It was rebuilt in 1859 in the Gothic style, with half the cost being provided by the maltster, Joseph Chuck. It is now the Leaside Church, which includes the United Reformed Church and Ware's Methodists, and the building at the front of the photograph has been converted to flats.*

Schooldays

At the top of Musley Hill stands the oldest school building in Ware where teaching still takes place. Its history takes us back to a contentious period in the history of the town's education. It was built in 1857 by Mrs Elizabeth Moore Chuck in memory of her husband, Edward Chuck, a wealthy maltster who had been killed in a carriage accident. The Chuck Memorial School was an attempt to reform secondary education in the town, since the old grammar school in the churchyard provided poor teaching, was falling down - and was, in any case, partly occupied by a brewer. But it was not until 1890 that agreement was reached to establish the Ware Grammar School for Boys on Musley Hill. This lasted until 1906, when it was amalgamated with Hertford Grammar School under a plan which established a Girls' Grammar School in Ware. Thereafter, the little school on Musley Hill became in 1907 a junior school, in 1918 a central school and in 1932 an infants' school, which it still is.

228. *The boys of Ware Grammar School in 1891, with the Headmaster, Mr Walter New, M.A. Cantab and on his right his assistant, Mr Knott.*

229. *A Victory party for the pupils of Musley Infants' School in 1945.*

230. *The little school on Musley Hill in its days as Ware Grammar School.*

231. Miss Woodhead with the Sixth Form of Ware Grammar School for Girls in 1948, seated outside the back door of Amwell House.

232. Mrs Robinson with the Sixth Form of 1961-62.

233. *The front of Amwell House in the 1950s. After the Grammar School moved out to Presdales House, Hoe Lane, in 1965, the building became part of Ware College of Further Education. Some of the ancillary buildings were demolished and the two protruding wings of Amwell House were shorted to allow widening of the London Road.*

234. *The rear of Amwell House in the 1960s, looking much as it does today - although this is a view which can only be had from the modern buildings of Ware College.*

235. *Millbrook, one of the old parts of Ware Girls' Grammar School, demolished in 1965.*

236. *Presdales, the former home of the Sandeman and McMullen families, which became a secondary school in 1965.*

SENIOR & CENTRAL SCHOOL, WARE. SEPT. 1939

237. *The Ware Senior and Central School outside their classrooms in Bowling Road, seen in 1939. In the centre is Mr Albert ("Taffy") Evans, who retired in 1948 after 25 years as headmaster.*

238. *The school in Bowling Road, which had been built as the Christ Church National Schools in the 1860s, once again took junior and infant children in 1961, when the seniors moved out to the new Trinity Secondary School. Here is Christ Church J.M.I. in 1965 with Mr Arthur Blundell as headmaster. He retired in 1966 and was succeeded by Mr Gordon Westbrook, two places to the right of him.*

WARE CHRIST CHURCH J. M. & I. SCHOOL. 1965

239. *Ware's oldest school for younger children was the St. Mary's National Schools, founded in 1820, and moved to larger premises behind St Mary's in Church Street in 1844.   Our picture shows Class III of the Infants in 1908.   The buildings were gradually run down after the Second World War and their responsibilities taken over by St Catherine's in Park Road and St. Mary's Juniors and Kingshill Infants on the new Kingshill Estate.*

Opposite:

240. *The Class IV senior girls of Christ Church National Schools in 1914.   This class gained the title "Sewers' Band", because of their diligence in sewing comforts for the troops in Flanders.*
241. *The top class of Musley Juniors in the 1920s.*

Great Events

By now the reader will appreciate that Ware is a town of great historical and architectural interest. Despite the re-emergence in later centuries of its neighbour, Hertford, as an important borough - or perhaps because of that - the civic pride of Ware people remained strong. This was very much the case in the early part of the 19th century when the town was solidly radical in politics and saw Hertford as a bastion of Tory interests. Ware was in favour of parliamentary reform and its own newspaper, *The Ware Patriot,* argued the case for widening the franchise of Hertford, which it regarded as the Marquess of Salisbury's pocket borough. In the Reform Bill election of 1832, the bargees and malting labourers of Ware marched into Hertford and did battle in the streets with the Marquess's henchmen. And when the Bill was passed, 4000 people sat down to a celebration dinner in Ware High Street.

Street parties to celebrate great national events continued to be held in the town and proclamations continued to be read out from the front of the Town Hall, which had been built in 1827 as a corn market in a vain attempt to entice the dealers away from the Hertford market. In this chapter, we look at those parties and proclamations and also at the succession of annual festivities which have culminated in the modern Ware Week, held in early July.

242. *1700 people sit down to dinner in the High Street to celebrate the Golden Jubilee of Queen Victoria on June 21st 1887.*

243. *The Station Hotel decked out for Queen Victoria's Golden Jubilee.*

244. *John Stribling's engraving of the Reform Bill dinner, held in the High Street on July 25th 1832.*

WARE QUEEN'S JUBILEE.

TUESDAY, JUNE 21st, 1887.

EVENTS OF THE DAY.

Time		Prizes		
7 a.m.	Church Bells ring			
9	Quarter-mile Swimming Race, (over 16 years)	10/-	5/-	
9.30	Ditto ditto, (12 to 16 years)	10/-	5/-	
9.30	Church Bells ring			
10	Service in the Parish Church			
11	Service in Christ Church with Band			
12.30 p.m.	Church Bells ring			
1	Dinner in High Street for 1700 people. Christ Church Band playing			
3	Children meet at their respective Schools			
3	Quarter-mile open Race	5/-	2/6	
3.20	Hurdle Race, 200 yards, (men over 18 years)	5/-	2/6	
3.40	Ditto, ditto, (under 18 years)	5/-	2/6	
4	Tea for about 1600 Children			
4	Greasy Pole across river (opposite Old River)	5/-		
4	Tug of War for women, (married v single)	12/-		
4.20	Barge-horse Race, bare back, round the flags as staked	20/-	10/-	5/-
4.40	Blind-fold Jockey Race, 100 yards, (jockey to be over 10 years)	5/-	2/6	
5	Children march to Mr. Hammond's Field, headed by Band			
5	Pony Race, bare back, ½ mile, (under 13 2 hands)	20/-	10/-	5/-
5.20	Tug of War for men, (married v single)	15/-		
5.40	High Jump, open	5/-		
6	Long Jump, open	5/-		
6.20	Jumping in Sacks, 100 yards	5/-	2/6	1/-
6.40	Flat Race, 300 yards, (18 to 40 years)	5/-	2/6	
7	Ditto, 100 yards (over 40 years)	5/-	2/6	
7.20	Ditto, 200 yards, (under 18 years)	5/-	2/6	
7.40	Egg and Spoon Race for women, 100 yards, (over 18 yrs.)	5/-	2/6	1/-
8	Ditto, ditto, (under 18 years)	5/-	2/6	1/-
8.20	Obstacle Race	5/-	2/6	1/-
	Greasy Poles (without ropes), for Legs of Mutton.			
8.25	Prizes given away, at the Committee Tent on the Ground			
8.30	Church Bells ring			
9	"God save the Queen" sung in High Street, headed by Band			
9.30	Torchlight Procession and Bonfire			

SPORTS COMMITTEE.

S. Barker, T. Burgess, J. Cox, E. Dewbury, J. Edwards, C. Field, H. H. Gilbert,
S. Goodman, C. Goodman, T. Rookby, Robert Smith, J. Stephenson, A. Thorowgood,
R. Thorowgood.

G. W. Cooper, *Umpire.* H. H. Gilbert, *Starter.* T. Rookby and R. Thorowgood, *Judges.*

CHILDREN'S SPORTS' COMMITTEE.

A. Bannister, G. Collins, M. Heaver, E. Malin, J. Newberry, G. Pavey, W. H. Smith,
P. Thomas.

REGULATIONS.

The whole of the events are confined to residents in the town of Ware.

Persons intending to take part in these Sports must give their names to ROBERT SMITH or CHAS. FIELD, members of the Sports Committee, at any time before Monday, June 20th, until 4 p.m., and state for which event they intend to compete.

No Competitor will be allowed to take more than 2 prizes, but if two or more prizes of equal value are won by the same Competitor, he or she shall take the first in order on the Programme.

The above regulation will not apply to the Tug of War or Blindfold Jockey Race Competitions. A time being fixed for the start of each Competition, it will be kept as far as practicable. Competitors must be at the Committee Tent so minutes previous to the stated time for starting, or will be disqualified.

The races will be started by rifle.

Barge horses must have worked 6 months at barge work.

245.   *A postcard, with a portrait of the Queen on the reverse, giving the programme of events for the Golden Jubilee. The regulations for the sporting events say that they are confined to residents in the town of Ware, no competitor may take more than two prizes, "the races will be started by rifle" and that the barge horse race would be confined to horses which had worked for six months on barge work. Note that the church bells began ringing at 7 a.m.*

Queen Victoria's Golden Jubilee was an event celebrated in every town and village throughout the land. The British Empire was at the peak of its power and the 50 years of peace and prosperity over which the Queen Empress had reigned was an occasion for universal rejoicing. But it had a special significance for Ware. The acrimonious debate over the future of secondary education in the town had just been resolved and a subscription list had been opened for the new Ware Grammar School on Musley Hill. In the event, the appeal brought in cash and promises of a little under a thousand pounds, which was just enough to endow the new school.

246. *Another view of the Golden Jubilee dinner in the High Street. Note on the left the front of the Falcon Works at 49-51 High Street, where the Goodfellow family manufactured kiln wire for the floors of the malting kilns. Why there were so many United States flags on display, and what the banner at the top of the right-hand pole signified, we do not know.*

Opposite:

247. *Greeting the troops returning from the South African War in 1902. A plaque and memorial window were put in St Mary's Church to the five Ware men killed by the Boers.*

248. *The Postmen's Walk sets off from the High Street in 1901. It was a 21 mile course, to Buntingford and back.*

This page:

249. *To mark the Coronation of Edward VII, a dinner for old people was held on June 26th 1902 in the new Drill Hall, in Amwell End, built through the generosity of the Hanbury family of Poles.*

250. *An invitation to the Coronation Tea, held in the Western Meadow (another name for Deerfield) made available by Captain Richard Benyon Croft.*

CORONATION OF
HIS MAJESTY KING EDWARD VII.

WARE CELEBRATION.

Admit *John Akers*

To TEA,

Which takes place in the WESTERN MEADOW
*(New Road Entrance), kindly lent for the
occasion by Capt. R. P. Croft.*

Hon. Treas. **Mr. C. Cook.** Hon. Gen. Sec. **Mr. A. C. Squier.**

251. *Flags adorn the High Street for the Coronation of King George V in 1910.*
252. *Crowds gathering for the Coronation celebrations, including the straw-hatted girls of the*
      Grammar School.

253. *The Proclamation of George V from the Town Hall in May 1910.*
254. *Crowds listening to the proclamation stretched down the High Street.*

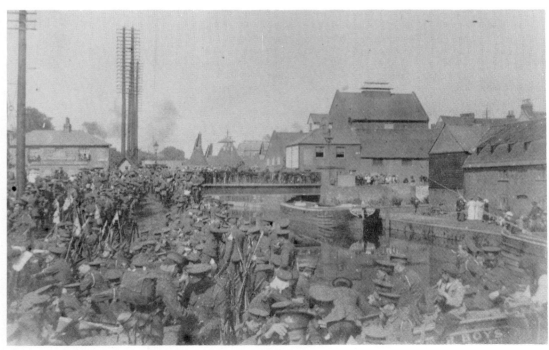

Ware in the First World War:

255. *Colonel Henry Page leading men of the Ware Territorial Battalion, 1st Hertfordshire Regiment, at Bridgefoot in 1914. They were in the B.E..F., the "Old Contemptibles".*
256. *The troops assembled on the towpath by Ware Bridge. The barge on the right was specially renamed "Our Boys" for the occasion.*

257. *During the First World War, the Priory was used as a hospital for convalescing soldiers. In the centre of the picture is the Medical Superintendent, Dr W.G. Stewart MBE.*
258. *The War Memorial to the 215 Ware dead, being unveiled on a wet day in June 1921.*

259. *The Proclamation of King Edward VIII, who later abdicated, in 1936.*
260. *A procession crossing the Bridge in the 1930s. Mystery surrounds the identity of the large banner. It may have belonged to a local organisation, like the Oddfellows, or been a trade union banner connected with the Jarrow Marchers, who came through Ware.*

261. *Ware's British Legion Carnival Queen, Betty Rayment, in 1939.*
262. *A float in a post-war carnival passing the Astoria Cinema in 1946.*

263. *Council workmen with the German landmine which fell at Ware Park in September 1941. It was attended by the Royal Navy, who declared it safe, and brought into Ware. When it was then found to be warm and ticking, the army took it to gravel pits in Watton Road and exploded it.*

264. *A Victory street party in Francis Road in 1945.*

265 and 266.   *The end of the Second World War - at least the end of the war against Hitler - was celebrated in most parts of the town with V.E. (Victory in Europe) parties.   These pictures show the grown-ups who prepared the V.E. Day party in Fanshawe Crescent in 1945 and the children who enjoyed it.*

Ware has had an annual fair or carnival since the Middle Ages. It was held at the beginning of September on the Feast of the Virgin Mary, to whom the parish church is dedicated, but fell into disuse at the end of the 19th century. Between the wars, the town held an annual British Legion Carnival in August and after the Second World War a Rose Festival was held, with the crowning of a Rose Queen. The modern successor to all these is Ware Week, which was inaugurated in 1970 and is now held in the first week of July. It begins with a carnival procession through the streets, with prizes awarded for the best floats. The Carnival Queen now goes under the title of "Miss Ware".

Opposite:

267. *The 1991 Miss Ware, Julie Wilson, with her attendant, Linda Brookes, photographed by the Hertfordshire Mercury with 14 former holders of the title Miss Ware.*

268. *A Ware Dramatic Society float in the Ware Week procession in the 1970s.*

Above:

269. *A Ware Week procession in the High Street in about 1980, photographed by a member of the Ware and District Photographic Society.*

270.   Cliff Richards and the Drifters on stage at the Astoria Cinema on Sunday July 6th 1958.

271.   Charles Ballands began working at the Astoria in Amwell End at the age of 13 and managed
       it for over 40 years until he died in 1974, aged 60.   He was a great independent cinema manager
       and innovator, and introduced live shows on stage.   Here he is in the late fifties with the Ware
       Salvation Army Guitar Group.

272. *Place House, the former medieval manor house of Ware, was restored in 1977 by the Hertfordshire Building Preservation Trust. The official opening was performed by the Queen Elizabeth, the Queen Mother, who is seen here greeting some of the disabled onlookers from Western House.*

273. *The celebration of the Queen Mother's 80th birthday coincided with the celebrations in Ware of 600 years since the building of the present Parish Church. For the occasion, a First Day Cover was issued by Ware Post Office.*

Ware People

Our final chapter celebrates the town's greatest asset, its people. Many of the rich and the famous have originated in Ware - Abbot Richard of Westminster, the poets William Vallans, Sir Richard Fanshawe and John Scott (who also built a grotto), the Revd. Charles Chauncy, one of the early presidents of Harvard, Caleb Hitch, the inventor of a type of industrialised building - to name but a few. But it is the ordinary townspeople whom we celebrate here for they contribute most to the special character of the town. Inevitably, they gather together in clubs, organisations and societies, with which Ware is plentifully supplied. Here are but a few of them.

274. *The Ladies of the Ware Inner Wheel - their equivalent of the Rotary - photographed in June 1962.*

275. *A party at Wickham's, with Mr Loxley Ford, Works Manager, fifth from the right.*

276. *In July 1955, the members of the Ware Urban District Council played the council staff at cricket. Our picture shows John Fletcher, late Clerk to Ware Town Council, tossing a coin for Dr. W.G. (Bill) May to call, with some familiar though youthful faces behind them.*

277. *The Specials of the Hertfordshire Constabulary "A" Division, who served throughout the Second World War from 1939-45.*

278. *A British Legion Dinner in 1946.*

279. *The members and cadets of the Ware Division of the St. John Ambulance Brigade, photographed with their Medical Officer, Dr Bill May.*

280. *First aid practice by the St John's. Crouching in front is Fred Woodhouse, who became Divisional Superintendent, and watching is Dr May.*

281.   Ware Brass on stage for a concert at Croydon, in the 1950s.

282.   A group of workers in the canteen of French's "Frenlite" mill in the 1960s.

283. *A famous Ware character, "Billy No Hat", photographed in the stocks at Great Amwell. He had the reputation of being a simple character but, when offered the choice between a sovereign (the gold pound coin) and a large old penny, he said he would take the smaller coin so as not to seem greedy.*

284. *John Rogers, who kept a shoemaker's shop in Baldock Street, from the end of the 19th century until 1936, was another Ware character. Unlike his respectable brother, the magistrate and printer A.H. Rogers, John specialised in the low life of the town, collecting items of gossip and folklore. He was the author of the poem (reprinted from time to time in the local newspapers) which names all the licensed premises in the town and begins:*

> It's said there are some Pubs in Ware.
> Well, yes, there are a few.
> This is the place where Malt was made
> So why not taste the Brew?

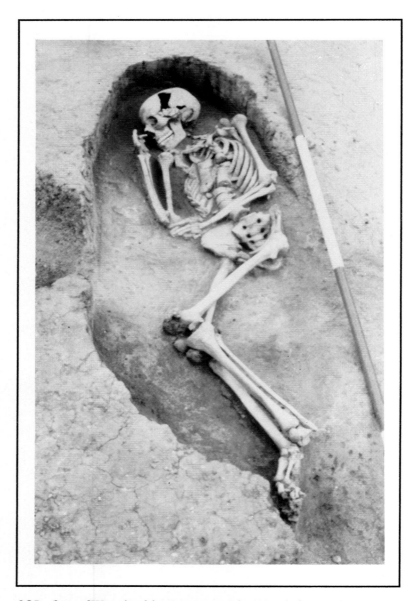

285. *One of Ware's oldest townspeople - the skeleton of a teenage girl, with extraordinarily fine teeth, excavated at the Glaxo's site beside Roman Ermine Street. Consequently, the archaeologists called her "Ermintrude".*

Index

192